Hospice Chaplain, *Interrupted*

Hospice Chaplain, *Interrupted*

The Postmodern Poems of a Spiritual Caregiver

C. SCOTT KINDER-PYLE

RESOURCE *Publications* · Eugene, Oregon

HOSPICE CHAPLAIN, INTERRUPTED
The Postmodern Poems of a Spiritual Caregiver

Resource Publications
An Imprint of Wipf and Stock Publishers
199 W. 8th Ave., Suite 3
Eugene, OR 97401

www.wipfandstock.com

PAPERBACK ISBN: 979-8-3852-3957-3
HARDCOVER ISBN: 979-8-3852-3958-0
EBOOK ISBN: 979-8-3852-3959-7

07/07/25

All artwork created by the author.

"Saint Judas" from COLLECTED POEMS © 1971 by James Wright. Published by Wesleyan University Press. Used by permission.

In memory of *John de Velder*, and in appreciation of *Unyong Statwick* and all Clinical Pastoral Educators, who curate the dark emotions.

With affection, empathy and compassion for colleagues everywhere and especially for *Robert, Mark, Lauren, Layne* and *Margot*, who during the Coronavirus Epidemic, interrupted the interruption by my side.

Contents

Acknowledgments | xi
~~Chaplin | 1~~
Essay: An Interruption to Lived Belief | 3
Introduction | 5
Lived Belief | 7
Philosophical Interruption | 12

Poems

I. Memory (Loss)

Abdomen-Smear | 27
Revisions for Logos | 30
The Reconnaissance of Whale-Speak | 31
Body Off the Dishman Hills Trail | 32
Jennersville Exit | 34
Per the Syllabus | 36
Signature Story | 37
Already Been Chewed | 39

II. Self Awareness

Reformed Silence, Always Reforming | 43
Steps in the Inter-Faith Direction | 45
I Made An Effort Last Spring at Prepping the Earth | 47

CONTENTS

Helpless Craving | 48

Paired with An 'Approachable' Wine | 49

Horseradish | 50

Middling | 52

Guided Tour | 54

Conjugation, 1985 | 55

Transgender Spy Agency | 56

III. Being Hospitable to Grief

The Unruly Cogito-On-Board | 61

Contrary to Theory | 63

Synchronized Fire-Setting | 64

Smoking Helps You Think | 65

A Boat Bought with a Hole In It Becomes a Memory,
     and Works Just Fine | 66

Emotional Purge | 68

Chaplain@Uvula | 70

IV. Not-Knowing

Asymptomatic Carriers | 79

Hitchcock Blonde | 80

Bottle Dance | 81

A Prayer for the Young Dead Who Never . . . | 82

Inhibition Lost | 83

Neuropathy Eventually | 85

Mudslides | 87

Hospice Chaplain, Interrupted | 88

CONTENTS

V. An Open-Ended Sort of Closure

Estate Sale for the Neurologically Disordered | 95

Spoiled | 97

Akedah Redux | 99

Butt Dial | 101

How We'll Age Together's Hard to Know | 102

To All the Corpses Still Bestowing the Secret Great
    Commission | 104

Baptizing Sturgeon | 105

(Or Does It?) | 107

Bibliography and Works Cited | 109

Acknowledgments

My gratitude to the editors of the following literary journals continues as the story of this chaplain unfolds, becomes interrupted and interrupts. Many thanks.

"Contrary to Theory" appeared in *Convivium* (2020, Volume 5).

"Horseradish" received honorable mention for the 2019 Anna Davidson Rosenberg Award, published in Poetica Magazine.

"Synchronized Fire-Setting" appeared in Pensive: A Global Journal of Spirituality and the Arts (2020).

"Spoiled" and "Jennerville Exit" appeared in Book of Matches (2022).

"The Reconnaissance of Whale-Speak" appeared in the *Sand Hills Literary Magazine* (2022).

"I have been close enough, and deranged by pain enough, to conclude that one is not always responsible for one's last acts, nor are they always worth interpretation."

—CHRISTIAN WIMAN, MY BRIGHT ABYSS

Chaplin

In the silent scene I'm watching
(the words coming afterwards)
that funny old comic
with his twitchy mustache
makes peace
while losing his hat
(perhaps a brimmed yarmulke)
in a wind gust. It spirals away from earth
toward outer darkness, and
every bleary-eyed mourner
watches it ascend.

I wish I could call you *friend*
and laugh the night away
sipping scotch,

but you're more precursor,
my mumbling bursar
at the pinnacle
of temple after temple . . .

my self-emptying
mimic and mime. Will you

interrupt ~~God~~

without saying
Excuse me?

Essay: An Interruption to Lived Belief

Moving into the field now, it becomes clearer to many practitioners, researchers and policy-makers that religion, belief, faith and spirituality are lived experiences and therefore, we are unable to generalize knowledge the way we thought or hoped we could.[1]

—Panagiotis Pentarisp

The certainty of death is the earnestness; its uncertainty is the instruction, the practice of earnestness. The earnest person is the one who through uncertainty is brought up to earnestness by virtue of certainty.[2]

—Soren Kierkegaard

It is not by superlatives that we can think of God, but by trying to identify the particular inter-human events that open towards transcendence and reveal the traces where God has passed.[3]

—Emmanuel Levinas

1. Pentaris, Panagiotis. Religious Literacy in Hospice Care: 189
2. Three Discourses on Imagined Occasions. Essential Kierkegaard: 167
3. Levinas, Face to Face: 32

FUNERAL ARRANGEMENT

INDICATE NAME OF CHURCH / HOUSE OF WORSHIP CHOSEN:

Required

Previous | History | Next

INTRODUCTION

I've got a problem with Hospice. And it's a big problem in that I work as a chaplain for a local Hospice organization. The problem is that I'm *so certain* about what I'm supposed to do that it frightens me. I'm frightened because, in that cosmic Venn diagram of interlocking spheres—the one depicting the overlap of *Terminally-Ill*, the *Religious*, and those patients likely to receive *Chaplaincy Care*—my work careens off the slopes of each arching line. I do what I'm supposed to do, which is offer a compassionate presence, listen actively for emotions related to a particular life context and chart any religious or non-religious affiliations. Nurses, bath aides and administrators call upon me to support them through some fairly messy existential crises, and I'm glad to help. But, at the end of the day, and into the night insomnia, I know that I've bracketed aside something crucial to being a Hospice chaplain; and that is the sheer mystery of death.

How could I miss it? It's been there in every hand-holding, in every halting articulation of profound loss, and in the faces of family and friends who remain at bedsides until the bitter end . . . and even among those who won't be there. Indeed, death may be easily defined as the cessation of those bodily functions necessary for a living organism to survive. But when a person with a life-narrative ceases to animate and perpetuate that story, I make haste to record the details of all that *can* be known while pushing to the margins all that *cannot* be known. Mystery! In the numerous coordination-notes written for my colleagues—for physicians, nurses, aides, administrators and corporate policy-makers—the enigma of the

5

deceased, but once-living, person is always inconvenient to mention and irretrievably lost.

This essay ventures the demise of that sort of compartmentalization, which is to say, I'm going to *unsay* some of things which have always been said; and I'm going to muster up the courage to think the thought that *cannot* really be thought. Namely, I'll be taking a stab at unraveling the cavalier and often strident ways that end-of-life caregivers cope with the repeated and close-up encounters they have with death, and with the dying. And I'll suggest, for good measure, how a chaplain might respond to the recent work of thanatologist Panagiotis Pentaris, who decries how the "lived belief" of the terminally-ill patient has gone missing from Hospice care for decades.

Let's begin with the last, first: as remedy to what ails us, the author of *Religious Literacy in Hospice Care; Challenges and Controversies* refers to a model for professional/patient interaction, a model that includes "the phenomenological appreciation" of religious, nonreligious or irreligious beliefs. He writes:

> "I am more interested in exploring how hospice professionals can facilitate faith as a concept which helps people make sense of their experience, rather than how religiously informed demands or preferences are addressed. I am aware that such a statement may not be well received by all disciplines and sciences, but I appreciate that it is open to debate."[1]

1. Pentaris: 137

6

LIVED BELIEF

Perhaps the debate anticipated by Pentaris is the one that pits the business-oriented, outcomes-based model—one which categorizes a patient's spiritual resources according to established religious traditions—against a posture which might allow the patient to arrive at a conceptual belief which cannot be necessarily traced to a particular branch of Christianity, Judaism, Islam, Hinduism, Buddhism, Paganism, etc.

Receiving this 'baton' in full stride, however, I'm inclined to take the following statement a little bit further: "We ought to consider deconstructing what we know or think we know, and learn anew."[1] Indeed. By all means. Without hesitation. Let's do this. And yet, if our efforts at deconstructing conventional beliefs or metaphysical opinions only lead the individual care-recipient toward the construction of another, perhaps more nuanced and idiosyncratic, set of beliefs and opinions, we may find ourselves, as caregiving professionals, succumbing to another version of "a very deeply-seated corporate neurosis"[2]—one that dates back to the earliest Christians communities' response to persecution under the Roman Empire. Faith *as a concept* is a misnomer; and a *lived belief* which becomes fixed or crystallized in the minds of caregiver or care-recipient may actually inhibit the on-going and open-ended wonder of facing *the Infinite* or *the Eternal*.

Having expressed that, I'm immediately distracted by the obvious *post-Christendom* and *post-secular* contexts in which these very words may have come to signify all that condescends,

1. Pentaris: 188
2. Shanks, Andrew. *What is Truth? Towards a Theological Poetics*: 6

patronizes, inflicts violence and traumatizes the very individuals a chaplain like myself is trying to soothe. Despite the well-known origins of the Hospice movement—and thank God for Cicely Saunders[3]—a commonplace vernacular of spirituality is increasingly hard to come by. Moreover, if *I* as your chaplain, identify myself as an ordained minister in the Presbyterian Church (USA), and if you apprehend through observation that I am a white, heterosexual, sys-gender male with an affinity for Philadelphia sports teams, that I am married, with two adult children, I'm gambling that my rapport with you will develop *either* because we share certain experiences and commitments . . . *or* because we don't . . . Either way, our rapport is not ultimately the point. Is it?

Chaplaincy, I would argue, engenders a more authentic trust when that gamble is all but lost, and when what remains between the caregiver and the care-recipient is the *absence* of certitude. Its lack. Its severance. Its vacuity in the face of what comes next. And what comes next cannot be spoken to anyone's satisfaction; moreover, if there are persons who assert that a metaphysical opinion *ought* to satisfy, I would argue it's the chaplain's job to disabuse them of this satisfaction.

Among my day-to-day, least favorite, activities as chaplain is the fidgeting I do with my computer tablet. Downloaded upon it is a software application, entitled, *PointCare,* and it's with this program's algorithms that my terminally-ill patients are rendered. They are rendered, for my purposes as chaplain, as *coping well* with their grief. Or perhaps they are *burdened* by unresolved issues, dilemmas regarding the forgiveness of a family member, the refusal to accept their diagnosis. But of all the boxes this chaplain must click with a finger-swipe, the one that perplexes me the most is the drop-down blank screen where the prompt asks for the *Patient's Spiritual Strength.*

Hmmm.

It's not that I'm devoid of possible answers. In nearly all my encounters, there are profound inner-resources that I've seen brought to bear, and these include a willingness to pray, a penchant

---

3. British Medical Journal. 2005 Jul 23;331(7510):238.

for quiet meditation, an abiding sense of humor, a capacity for expressing gratitude . . . and the list goes on. Believe me: I've rushed to fill in that barren space with more verbiage, more euphemistic sloganeering, more fideistic schtick, than I care to admit. Nonetheless, are we talking about the limitations of a mortal existence, of a consciousness who is coming to the edge and peering over? I'm not necessarily referring to the standard belief in *life-after-death*. I'm not even talking about the protoplasmic energy that's potentially released into the stratosphere when a personality wafts away. I'm simply pondering the benefits to the patient of not-knowing-for-sure.

And yes, if such *benefits* endure and extend to the patient's family members, friends, or to anyone else who mourns, would that be a strength? A weakness? An indication of the dreaded *bereavement risk*?

Or would the best way to demarcate a mortal being's brush with (possible or impossible) immortality be a series of open-ended questions, self-interrogations, struggles, wrestlings, the kinds of emotions that comprise Rudolph Otto's *mysterium tremendum* . . .

Pentaris, through his research among Hospices in the United Kingdom, suggests that *religious literacy* is not a matter of comprehending all the tenets, rituals and assorted practices of the world's religions or belief systems; his point is well-taken. Individuals, at the end-of-life, have their anguish compounded by various "micro-invalidations, G and it's these faux pas which chaplains may remedy directly or indirectly merely by saying 'I don't know.' That is, by guiding conversation beyond the propositional truth-claim, i.e., what one is supposed to believe, and by daring to venture into territories which are ambiguous and untamed by the life-narrative, chaplains may abandon the stereotypical technical-fix of rescuing the bereft with their piety.

I recall reading a poem by James Wright, entitled *Saint Judas*, and how my appreciation of it performed wonders. The poem adopts the first-person perspective of the infamous betrayer of Jesus, whose soul's ultimate condition had been my tradition's foregone conclusion. Masterfully, the poet takes that theological rush-to-judgment into account, assuming that Judas is suicidal for all the right reasons. Might there be a hospice patient, estranged from the Christian faith, who begins to feel strangely liberated by the sonnet's final stanza? And yet, what is the *lived belief which makes sense of the experience?* I would argue there is none.

On the contrary, as Wright holds space for both chaplain and patient and perhaps aggrieved survivor, the coherence of a belief may be the very thing to be relinquished in the name of authentic care. Moreover, the presumption of the traditional narrative is not rejected or subjected to disrespect, but somehow held in abeyance.

Saint Judas

When I went out to kill myself, I caught
A pack of hoodlums beating up a man.
Running to spare his suffering, I forgot
My name, my number, how my day began
How soldiers milled around the garden stone
And sang amusing songs; how all that day
Their javelins measured crowds; how I alone
Bargained the proper coins, and slipped away.

Banished from heaven, I found this victim beaten,
Stripped, kneed, and left to cry. Dropping my rope
Aside, I ran, ignored the uniforms:
Then I remembered bread my flesh had eaten,
The kiss that ate my flesh. Flayed without hope,
I held the man for nothing in my arms.[4]

The point I wish to make in citing this verse is the same point a *phenomenological appreciation* of knowledge tends to make *if* the parameters of this philosophical outlook are taken seriously. Namely, the holding of "the man for nothing in my arms" is equivalent to the possibility that *all* persons are perpetual mysteries both to themselves and to others. For the professional caregiver to then omit that enigmatic element simply because it's difficult to quantify or to qualify would be a profound blunder, and perhaps

---

4. Wright, Selected Poems: 140.

one that might jeopardize the integrity of the care that's purportedly being offered.

My insight is not merely that people's beliefs undergo change and defy categorization but that the chaplain who interrupts a settled belief with an 'I wonder about that' may prompt a moment of profound truth-telling. The chaplain who interrupts with a comment to the effect of 'You seem unsure about your belief here. How does that feel to you?' may usher in a much-needed nuance or equivocation.

Sallie Tisdale, in an article for the March/2018 issue of *Harper's* magazine, describes her encounters with a variety of Alzheimers' patients. As a sensitive nurse and as an observant writer Tisdale describes some fascinating observations, and among them is the unlikely prognosis that persons, suffering with dementia, are *not* necessarily unhappy, but experience rather "a rare entrancement with their surroundings, a simplicity of perception, a sense of wonder."[5] Moreover, despite the fact that a particular patient in her care had been known as a prim and proper Presbyterian housewife, she started lifting up her shirt in public and cursing at us. She hid money in the oven, and in the last months of her life would lie on the floor, arms outstretched, talking loudly. To her family, she seemed to be a different person—not our mother anymore. But I had known her only as an adult; I'd seen her sharp edges in a way her children could not. When the skein of the past unravels, so does repression. The housewife lets the world finally hear the complaints she has been mumbling to herself all along.[6]

Uncertainty abounds. And it abounds especially with regard to personal identity. Tisdale refers to contemporary scholars Daniel Dannett and Paul Broks in framing her questions: "Is consciousness a story? Is it story, author, and reader as one?" The answer, despite the obvious memory-loss associated with dementia-patients, appears to be matriculating in the affirmative direction. But what might the anxious or resolute anticipation of death, and the coming alongside of the dying, mean for such storytelling? Its completion? (Who's reading then?)

5. Tisdale. "Out of Time." *Harpers*, Mar. 2018.

6. Ibid

Philosophical Interruption

To be discovered in mostly every Hospice visit is a narrative center of gravity, which appropriates things, events, places and most critically, other persons, as a creative enterprise. Irrespective of, and yet coincidental with, the involuntary and vital functioning of the physical brain, the inner-dialogue of self-consciousness veers into public space, and in so doing maps the unruly stimuli into a coherent whole . . .

Until it doesn't.

Eventually, and perhaps *inevitably*, chaplains must come to terms with what Tisdale articulates. The story of a person's existence cannot be measured adequately by demographics. Nor is it *understood* per se in the same ways clinicians understand the co-morbidities which will culminate with the cessation of life. Soren Kierkegaard, for instance, after chronicling levels of human existence in terms of the *Aesthetical, the Ethical* and the *Religious*, writes,

> It is quite true what Philosophy says: that Life must be understood backwards. But that makes one forget the other saying: that it must be lived—forwards. The more one ponders this, the more it comes to mean that life in the temporal existence never becomes quite intelligible, precisely because at no moment can I find complete quiet to take the backward position."[1]

Of course, the *forwards* aspect remains a conundrum for the terminally-ill patient, who is invited to give thanks for peak experiences, who is celebrated for meeting familial and ergonomic

1. Kierkegaard. Diary: 98.

obligations, and yet who cannot get outside of himself to register the completion of a life-narrative. Clumsily, chaplains may try and fail, and every attempt at validation is undoubtably worth the effort.

And yet, what about the transcendence which is being alluded to, or maneuvered around (in denial)? Curiosity regarding this patient's *lived belief* entails an appreciation for both the facts and figures which can be known, measured and recorded for posterity . . . *and* those aspects of a person's narratability which will never be known in full, if at all. "Certainty is the greatest of illusions," writes neuroscientist Iain McGilchrist:

> whatever kind of fundamentalism it may underwrite, that of religion or of science, it is what the ancients meant by *hubris*. The only certainty, it seems to me, is that those that believe they are certainly right are certainly wrong . . . A leap of faith is involved for scientists as much as for anyone.[2]

Apart from *anyone,* therefore, this essay now pivots on the question of *Why.* That is, why might the patient who does *not* believe in anything approaching *life-after-death* still want, or become curious enough, to consider *a leap of faith* even *as* the content of that *faith* were emptied of propositional truth-claims? For an answer, we must do what the School of Phenomenology has taught us to do since Edmund Husserl [1859–1938] and Martin Heidegger [1889–1976]. And we must then peruse the critique, or the rupture to, that school's expository strategies, as inspired by Emmanuel Levinas [1906–1995].

Husserl's approach, for example, would pursue *apodictic* knowledge by placing in figurative brackets all that might be *justifiably doubted.* "Despite all this," he writes, "we come to understandings with our neighbors, and set up in common an objective spatio-temporal fact-world."[3] So, then comes the chaplain's dilemma. If *I*—the originating self-consciousness—encounter

2. McGilchrist. The Master and its Emissary: 460

3. As quoted in *Phenomenology: The Philosophy of Edmund Husserl . . . ,* by Joseph Kockelmans: 73

another human being in that 'fact-world,' I must still remain ever and always uncertain as to that person's *lived belief*, which has not be 'set up in common . . .'

Consequently, under the Husserlian scheme, any information pertaining to that slippery territory is rendered irrelevant and out-of-bounds. That such would become the predictable result for Hospice caregivers prompts the foreground for both indifference as well as supposed neutrality. That is, when the terminally-ill patient or an involved family member communicate their grief in halting sentences—even word-salad sentences—chaplains are prone to look elsewhere for the material that seems more clear-headed and coherent. By doing so, however, I run the risk of encapsulating both the patient and the family into the world as only *I, and my bio-medical colleagues,* understand it. Something of the patient's radical *Otherness* goes missing.

Likewise, as Heidegger's magnum opus, *Being and Time*, spindles down from the complicit heights of this thinker's Nazi-party affiliation, the affable and always-available chaplain may project upon the care-recipient the very cultural and historical values which are in vogue. Given such a mindset—in which everyone is 'spiritual' in some way—or in which every spirituality is a ruse to be exploited by those in power—the patient becomes the victim of broad, hegemonic generalizations. Writes Heidegger: "Being-in-the-World is disposed to 'take things' in some way, to suppose, to be certain, to have faith—a way of behaving which itself is always a founded mode of Being-in-the-world." [250][4]

All this, of course, smacks of elitist and esoteric thinking, but it's by thinking about phenomena through and through . . . to the edge of what can be known, that Levinas enters the fray and provides a respite. Unlike Husserl, whose self-consciousness is utterly autonomous, and unlike Heidegger, whose self-consciousness is already embedded in world history, Levinas emphasizes that which might be *otherwise—Otherwise than Being*[5]—and for chaplains in

4. Heidegger. *Being and Time*: 293

5. Levinas' major work, published in 1974, in which the author writes, "I am answerable before the other in his alterity . . . To be responsible before

whose care persons sometimes speculate on *what's next,* there is something refreshingly honest in approaching each individual as bounded by an alterity which will never be breached and which permits authentic relationships without enmeshment. He writes in *Time and the Other*:

> Properly speaking, neither the other Ego himself, nor his subjective processes or his appearances themselves, nor anything else belonging to his own essence, becomes given in our experience originally. If it were, if what belongs to the other's own essence were directly accessible, it would be merely a moment of my own essence, and ultimately he himself and I would be the same.[6]

Again, by highlighting the dangers of the *same,* Levinas speaks to the heart of the contemporary Hospice movement. According to Pentaris, this movement endeavors to care for persons of diverse religious, nonreligious, irreligious, faith or no-faith backgrounds. As professionals are trained in this manner and set out to honor the differences they face, any expression from patients which lacks clarity or which fail to coalesce around the collective wisdom of what constitutes *comfort*, any sense of existential angst, becomes a problem to be solved.

As chaplain then, what am I called to do?

Do I conform to the *same* agenda which subsumes patients under the banner of managing their grief? Do I hang my hat at the doorway of the bereaved spouse, ex-spouse, child or step-child, and lump them together according to how many times each one declares 'I'm fine'? Or does the finite collide with the infinite at the very moment when I, as chaplain, allow all that is unmanageable in the situation to become situated at bedside?

None of these inquiries is intended to promote (beyond the family's own attachments) anything close to a proselytizing remark or a manipulative shedding of tears. Rather, what I intend is what the *phenomenological appreciation* of my knowledge intends for me—which is an appreciation of the (Im)possibilities.

another is . . . to put oneself in his place." [xx].

6. Levinas: Time and the Other: 108

Now, at the risk of hyperbole or overstatement, evidence of the extremes are obvious. In one story, a little girl named Olive had passed away suddenly, which left her mother, a megachurch's lead singer, utterly distraught. As a means of coping with the tragic loss, however, this grief-stricken parent declared, "Olive's time here is not done," and proceeded to call upon her fellow worshippers to pray for her bodily resurrection. She then enlisted the support of some 250,00 *Instagram* followers to do likewise. Not to be out-done, the pastor delayed the funeral for the two-year-old, saying, "How can God choose not to heal someone when he's already purchased the healing?" The saga then came to an end as the body's decomposition recalibrated expectations, and the *GoFundMe* site helped to defray costs for Olive's family . . . [7]

About a year prior to this debacle, Father Don Lauesta had been delivering a homily in Temperance, Michigan, where a teenager had taken his own life. The priest, it seems, took the opportunity to then muse about the fate of those persons who throw away God's most precious gift. And before the weeping congregation, he debated aloud whether or not this suicide victim would be welcomed into heaven. "Father, please!" a parent intervened. But with the authoritative voice sometimes ceded to men in white collars and black frocks, a religious certitude rang out and confirmed the worst of what beliefs in the afterlife can do . . . [8]

Levinas, for all his obtuse language, would have none of this. His phenomenology creates an atmosphere in which theists, atheists and agnostics may not—as the old adage goes—'agree to disagree'—but agree about that which cannot be known with certainty. Is it likely that chaplains, who've been schooled in the art of belief, will stop themselves? Or will I, as one of them, simply speak from the epicenter of my own lived belief (which is still in process) while allowing others the same privilege? Suppose one precludes the other. Suppose, for instance, an ardent believer is

7. Ramsey, "There's No Shame When a Miracle Doesn't Come," *Christianity Today* (December 27, 2019).

8. See Edward N. Peters' in "God bless Fr. LaCuesta," *The Catholic World Report* (December 17, 2018).

dying of congestive heart failure and announces his steadfast conviction with his last remaining breaths. Do I interject with my lack of certitude? Do I call out what to me may be delusional thinking about grand reunions in the seventh heaven? About a cataclysmic last battle on earth? About seventy virgins awaiting the deceased in Paradise? About returning to the ecosystem as a dolphin?

I do not. I offer nothing but sighs in response to what the believer maintains as the truth that awaits . . . as I reply very little to that which induces the nonbeliever to scoff. What awaits, I can report, is the flip-side of finitude's play-list, and the 'songs' that have been sung include lyrics by the Aesthete, the Ethicist and the Religious. (Kierkegaard strikes again!). Moreover, as one's self-narrative as chaplain elides with that of the terminally-ill, Levinas rightly restores us to the common element:

> It is the living human corporeality, as a possibility of pain, a sensibility which of itself is the susceptibility to being hurt, a self uncovered, exposed and suffering in its skin. In its skin it is stuck in its skin, not having its skin to itself, a vulnerability. Pain is not simply a symptom of a frustrated will, its meaning is not adventitious. The painfulness of pain, the malady or malignity of illness (*mal*), and in the pure state, the very patience of corporeality, the pain of labor and aging, are adversity itself, the against oneself that is the self.[9]

Visceral 'goosebumps' here are all but required. And whether or not one resonates with every translated (from French) syllable, I see and I feel and I taste and I smell and I hear . . . the stuff of Pentaris' *lived belief*. More to the point, I sense the vulnerability with which chaplains are called upon to come alongside the terminally-ill—and *without* the religious overlay!

As pastor, in preparations for a funeral once, I took into my hands *The Book of Common Worship* and went about the work of asking the deceased person's family about her life. In my tradition, *A Service of Witness to the Resurrection of Jesus Christ* includes a liturgical statement, "In the sure and certain hope of the resurrection

9. Levinas. Otherwise than Being: 51

. . . ,Ġ and I recall uttering these syllables before a gathering of the bereaved, which included a eclectic range of theists, atheists and agnostics. Yet, just as I retrieved the name of the matriarch who had died at age 92—her name was in fact *Shirley*, (and I've received permission to use it)—the dialogue from the 1980 film, *Airplane!*, intruded upon my thoughts.

Yikes! For those unfamiliar with the particular exchange I had in mind, it involved a character, played by Leslie Nielsen, who is desperately trying to convince, another character, played by Robert Hays, that he should pilot a massive Boeing 707 to a safe landing. "Surely you can't be serious" was the set-up line. And in reply, Nielsen's character says, "I am serious. And don't call me Shirley . . . "

Imagine my professional embarrassment; and although nothing untoward escaped my lips, I found my homily strangely affected by the very real possibility that the deceased, a woman known by the name *Shirley*, was entirely *Different* than whomever I, or anyone else at the gathering, had presumed her to be. That is, in her death, her *face* had spoken otherwise.

For times like these, Levinas also employs the word *diachrony* as opposed to *synchrony*, and his point, it seems to me, is that each person we encounter is not simply a person, found within a sequence or within a succession of moments, days, weeks, months years or centuries; but there is a finite instant through which one becomes conscious of straddling the line beyond which there is no measurable duration of time—the *Infinite*. This, I'll admit, can be a sobering, if not a devastating, thought. In fact, given the ephemeral span in which human beings do their (best and worst) thinking, it can scarcely *be* thought. And yet, beyond the contemplation of paradox, the *Infinite* has resonance as the flip-side of the finite playlist which will eventually run out of theme-songs. Ideally chaplains, who developed ears for such music, will wait . . . and wait, but wait for what? More music? Angelic symphonies? The sacred *Om* of the Universe? For chaplains, as for any person who cultivates a sensitivity to the positive and negative influences of religion in society, the event of the other person's death's tends to bifurcate the belief-options.

On the subject of how to conduct the funeral, for example, one of my old professors, Thomas G. Long offers the standard in liturgics for clergy:

> If the biography of the deceased is the only sacred story we know how to tell, the death, which has brought this story to its sad end, wins again, and no measure of our remembering and comforting each other can push back that grim truth. Only the resurrection story unmasks death's fraud. Only the story of resurrection stakes out a victory over death, and this holy script needs to be told and performed again and again at funerals.[10]

The only question is—does it? Should it? Among Christians, I will affirm and applaud the theological orthodoxy. But inasmuch as I serve predominately today as chaplain, there is something disingenuous and disrespectful (to the tradition itself) when I presume that *all* of my listeners accept, and *ought to believe* in "the resurrection story." And, as I've indicated above, there are increasingly a number of popular ways of acknowledging the Infinite with a wink and a nod . . . and then averting one's gaze with a turn back toward the rich tapestry of finitude.

In fact, as I had wrestled psychically with my *Shirley* service, contemporary philosopher, Martin Hagglund, was beginning his book tour of the United States. I bought the book, and in *This Life; How Mortality Makes Us Free*, there is found this juxtaposed set of beliefs:

> A religious faith cannot add anything to the dignity and pathos of mourning; it can only subtract from the mourning by diminishing the sense of loss. This is not to say that avowedly religious people do not mourn. But insofar as they do mourn, their mourning is animated by a secular faith in the irreplaceable value of a finite life rather than by a religious faith in eternity. If you truly believe in the existence of eternity—and in the superior

10. Long. Accompany Them with Singing: 137.

value of eternal life—there would be no reason to mourn the loss of a finite life."[11]

Informed primarily by Levinas, a phenomenological appreciation of these polemical views might filter out the drive for certitude, and allow the vigorous debate over "religious faith" versus "secular faith" the appropriate context—which is *not* front and center. Arguments as to the rightness or wrongness of belief or skepticism require humility and equivocation. Indeed the moments leading up to and surrounding the patient/chaplain encounter may resound with a cacophony of claims and counterclaims. Nonetheless, at the time of the face-to-face, there is little room for anything but what Richard Kearney calls "dispossessive bewilderment."[12] As chaplain I cultivate *bewilderment*, which is to say, I allow myself to feel *bewildered*, primarily because the face of the person before me demands it. That is, I feel my own story as a caregiving, empathetic sort of sojourner disrupted. Will he ask too much of me? Will her gibberish require more time than I seemingly have to decipher? Will their leaps in logic cause me to check out of the conversation?

Levinas scholar Colin Davis provides this proscription:

> The word face is an ordinary word . . . yet, having chosen such an ordinary word, Levinas then divests it of its common meanings . . . The face, in Levinas's account, should not be confused with the part of the head where the eyes, nose and mouth are to be found. In the face, the Other is presented to me directly and as utterly external to me . . . [13]

It's the face, and not the search for a patient's lived experience, that creates this indebtedness I feel. And yet, by employing the term, I join with Levinas in signifying the unique person who cannot be seen, the one who cannot be distinguished by eye-color, body-type or scars . . . The face connotes what no object

11. Hagglund. This Life: 62
12. Kearney. Anatheism: 17
13. Davis. Levinas: 132

in the room, and what no image on the screen can declare. Quite imaginatively, the philosopher gives to each face of the face-to-face interaction an impromptu script. The gist of the script might be construed as religious—Judaic—as in, "Thou shall not kill." Another variation on the Levinasian saying is, "Give me my place in the sun." But regardless, the inference for Hospice chaplains might be incredibly instructive.

Come hell or high water, hold space. Come dogma or desperation, hold space.

That is, allow for the differentiation of selves (caregiver and patient) to foment without distilling the dynamics down to the professional characterization alone. The fluidity of a lived belief must necessarily erode and corrode the very language that seeks to ossify it. And, therefore, it falls to the chaplain to provide nuance and to promote an authentic exchange in which one's imminent death is itself permitted its essential *Otherness*—which is to say, no living consciousness can bring that mystery within its orbit.

From this vantage point, practical knowledge and logistical analysis fade in the background; all that nitty-gritty work will of course happen, and chaplains have been charged with due-diligence to see that it's accomplished. But might there be an offering of hope in the mere acknowledgment of what eludes clinical analysis? Or will it be vanquished by the very religious role that seeks to honor such hope? Will it become crowded out by Hospice bureaucracies?

Chaplains, I submit, need not synchronize their watches or fine-tune their cellular devices.

Chaplains need not spend the *majority* of their time organizing day-calendars, or plotting their care-plans.

Chaplains need not assume that time is better spent with those who are more cognitively aware of themselves and their surroundings.

Instead and in conclusion, I propose the artistry of *interruption*. Each face-to-face with a patient epitomizes the very interruption of death that will inevitably come to the professional caregivers for Hospice. Rising like a mist from this much anticipated, much dreaded, interruption is the *lived belief* of unique persons who cannot and will never be fully known. And if that sounds too unequivocal, perhaps it is. What I mean to suggest is that all that passes for knowledge of places, things and events will not accommodate, summarize or exhaust knowledge of a human being's own first-hand experience. There is an enigma there that neither Hospice nor the long peccadillo of history can sweep into its incongruous categories.

But poetry helps!

###

Poems

I. Memory (Loss)

"The fiction of narrative
solitude is the poet's old
lie, and most of us
do it and those who do
know why. After all,
there's no one else here
now, on this near
isthmus of memory."

—Jonathan Johnson, from *In*

ABDOMEN-SMEAR

1. Lactose Intolerance

"You know
what would be good

with these?
Something I can't have."

2. Cough

When the last lozenge lodged
in the Stone-Henge-shaman's incantations
the new and improved ingredients
seemed to soothe the scratchiness
of solstice light

and I, dutiful and desperate, waited
until the boring mid-afternoon
for the phlegm hacked up
to anoint for myself
a flaming forehead.

3. Sketch of the Ephemeral

I kissed her with my tongue involved
and licked the graphite
clean off the page.

From this point forward,
you'll have to take my word
for her rare beauty.

4. Light Source

The lantern you're holding will be redundant
if the sun is shining

and the red army ants surrender
only to retreat
another day
into night.

But go ahead and enjoy
your 'roughing it'

experience.

5. Writing Process

. . . a sharpened stick
dipped in a lightening
bug's amber
abdomen-smear

. . . the sidewalk cement
emblazoned with glowing
aphorisms . . .

And yet . . .
with creatures sparser and unavailable

there are mangled bodies in the threads
of mayonnaise jars . . .

too numinous to mention.
And now

that I have your attention
by hastily screwing on
the lid,

a glory appears.

6. Body Image

With dying-visits nearly complete
my amygdala's bivouac
withdraws to a falling-down shack
usurped by fields of golden wheat.

7. If What's Been Said Has Any Merit

. . . and atoms from
your run-of-the-mill T-Rex
reside in us today,
I'm so on-board
with where they're headed next.

REVISIONS FOR LOGOS

In New Mexico
where I'd been only once

for a weekend—
staying at the *LaQuinta Inn*—

re-writing for Barbara
a curriculum that never saw

the light of day (or night)—
a giant sloth left footprints

juxtaposed to the primitive
humans who might've crossed

its path and would've speared the now-
extinct creature for food.

Over breakfast burritos with
salsa and sour cream the deceased

said she'd get back to me
with revisions.

The Reconnaissance of Whale-Speak

It bassoons in the tenor range where I'd be
the most frightened, at the murkiest depths:

 a sound so unlike my notorious breaths
 I'd conjure up the sinister scrutiny
 afforded the latest cohort of krill.

You may have guessed—I'm an inland
kind of human who'd rather the shrill
voices stick with the supply and demand
of more turf than melancholic surf.

 And you'd be right. Except for acoustics.

A song surveils my sleep and finds a dwarf
star surrounded by horrified hiccups.

 Any mammal with a blow hole fills the void—
 pilot whales, humpbacks, pregnant dolphins
 who surface addictions to celluloid.

And let the orcas, even with their predatory
instincts, find a groaning that violins
the long-awaited birth. No exculpatory
evidence will be forthcoming
to absolve the hook, net or harpoon.

 But the Behemoth will croon.
 And the strings will be strumming.

BODY OFF THE DISHMAN HILLS TRAIL

A writer said his career began with a dead body.
Mine wasn't how I pictured it:
inconspicuous
between two outcroppings
of basalt—and risen
up like a snowdrift
with vivisections
melting back into the meadow,
leaving legs, arms, torso
and a full head of undulating hair.

Come to think of it—
maybe it was a snowdrift after all.

Pocked with bits of moss-laden tree bark—
who could blame me?

A viscous fissure, a crimson coagulation
beginning to drip-drip-drip—
who could
blame me for seeing what I saw?

But dioramas be damned!
There's nothing papier-mâché
about boulders being moved aside.
However it happened.

And though the odds are slim
to none

my pace quickens at the thought:
a writing career—abandoned
because I saw a body
off the trail.

Jennersville Exit

The passenger in my mother's Monte Carlo
doesn't blow me like she implicitly promised.
That was long ago.

But having pulled to the same berm
off Route One, headed south,
I look for the clouds

to descend upon the ramp and have their way again and again.
A cumulous did in fact
back then,

and with its voluptuous haunches corralling my face,
from ear to ear, I heard the bridge of my nose unbuckle in a
breeze.

All was not well . . . mostly because I didn't comprehend
                                        at that time
                                        arriving now

at *Ye Ol' Red Rose Inn.* Grounded with gravitas,
coming by degrees, and by certain extra pounds
accrued in the Scotch-drinking phase of life—

I return to my nasal cavity's tickling toward consummation—
to the classic sneeze—

which may have been attributable
to manure from the local mushroom farms
had it not been for the stench of my own future corpse.

"You know, you know," I was saying to my paramour then (who
didn't know),
"God's like . . . " —and it blew— a plume of violent biome!

And like wartime flack it pock-mocked the windshield to where I
couldn't see.
I had said *Yeshua* , as if calling down fire . . . but nothing came to
mind
I wanted smitten for eternity.

Now as then, however, they parade out from nearby thickets. One
by one,
my posthumous works emerge as Hispanic migrants
often do. A few were, and are still, named *Hector.*

The others, *Jesus,* (pronounced *Hey-seus*) for sure.
And smiling, they peer through
the passenger window,

shading eyes, with hands cupped to foreheads
and squinting over the ample lap
of long-ago. "Dios lo bendiga,"
they can't resist saying.

Per the Syllabus

In memory & appreciation of John Haag

In the dumpster of my desk the files were found:
bloated with pages
the texture and pallor
of decrepitly thin skin,

layers upon layers
of manuscripts,

all still marked
in the margins
by you . . .

who
by now has deciphered
all that my ill-equipped poems
could never evoke.

> *I cannot, I will not,*
> *attempt to dispute*
> *revelation with you.*
> *Please abandon the homilies.*
> *Forsake the time-worn*
> *banalities.*
> *You assume your intentions*
> *will suffice*
> *in spite of*
> *the mediocrity*
> *of your language.*

SIGNATURE STORY

"Because I lie and sign myself to lies!"
—JOHN PROCTOR, *THE CRUCIBLE,* ACT IV

It proves
I've been communing
this whole time—
a sloppy signing
like hastily-stitched sutures
upon the seepage of a wound
where the 'y' is loosed
to effect a sort of ladle
for doling out the fish stew
which becomes the stagnant pond.

And it proves
I've been communing
this whole time
with the guy who painted eye-patched
buccaneers on the high seas
and who buried treasure
where 'x' marked the moniker
for a beloved buffoon in fictitious barracks.

Finally, it proves there were peasants
who pickpocketed royals (dressed like them
and addressed one another like them)—
and that from a frozen bog
they extracted their trinkets,
preserved in peat,

as well as their bodies
caught dead
and to their chagrin
hyphenated.

Already Been Chewed

After several attempts now
the petrified gum I mistook
for a rock in my boyhood
rock collection
has proven to be
a poor prompting
for my imaginative
prowess.

I've since resigned myself to the fact
that if I had mindlessly
stuck my *Wrigley's Spearmint*
beneath the ornate molding
of some nearly defunct
church pew
I could have gotten
more mileage out of it.

The D.N.A., for instance, might've
been mined like a rare-earth
mineral, and the genetic code
given a less generic
beginning in the womb
of some Singularity
who wouldn't know
a death rattle from
a *Bazooka* bubble.

II. Self Awareness

"Hours later, I thought of her
in her bed, on the morphine, the leukemia thriving
inside her bones. But soon again,
then, I was thinking about myself.
I can't seem to keep my mind on anyone
else . . . "

—SHARON OLD, FROM *HER LAST AUGUST*

Reformed Silence, Always Reforming

Just yesterday
a silence in the vestibule
scurried away and slipped through cracks
in the sanctuary
walls.

Taking it as a sign
I grabbed the sledgehammer
from among the stoles and albs
and went to work on the sheetrock.

Old sermon
illustrations, commentary
scraps had been transformed into a rat's nest;
and with the vermin no where in sight
I scanned the fragments for anecdotes.

The air inside the walls was thick
with rancid olive oil, burned-out votive
and Christ candles from generations ago;
I pulled my clerical collar over my mouth and nose.

Then tunneling
into another chamber I sequestered myself
as if behind a sepulcher where, it turns out,
the mildew left a fairly substantial
meal on the forgotten casserole dishes.

Dropping tools of the trade
I fingered the shape
of two women
running and veiled
in the flaky fungus.
As of yesterday
they had nothing yet to say.

Steps in the Inter-Faith Direction

with apologies to John Godfrey Saxe

No one has seen the whole elephant
(not even those with impeccable eye-
sight)

so we can't assume
its parts are
even parts of a whole.

Yes, I've come to an impenetrable wall.
You feel the threatening spear and find yourself jabbed
to the side. The snake writhes like a pachyderm's tail,
swatting those humongous flies on the African savanna.
The tree's firmly rooted in mud. It's hot and humid,
and so to experience the fan waft the air about's
a welcome relief. But as for the rope,
it's so thick and coarse, it may as well not
be a rope.

Damn it! Walk with me,
you comparative-
religions guru.

I've tracked succulent seeds
with the rubber tread of my loafers
into and out of the houses of the dead.

They've all been riding bicycles,
balancing on a sun-baked path.
One glances at the gaping wound, the other
away:

a bit of green's growing
in the dehiscence of earth.

I Made An Effort Last Spring at Prepping the Earth

Sending away for worms
to aerate the soil
came to nothing.

The cryogenically-stored
lady bugs release
came to nothing.

Steer manure,
purchased in bulk,
came to nothing.

Granules of nitrogen,
spread along the furrows,
came to nothing.

But thunderstruck,
with the sprinkling of your ashes,
my garden grew

the most gorgeous
mushrooms
out the yin and into the yang.

HELPLESS CRAVING

I had to drive through
Alabama once
to get to La Place
where I ate crawdads—
a bowlful of red thoraxes—
shelled in a pinch
and plunked in my suckling
mouth. I had to

to satisfy a craving

before leaving—
back through Alabama
where the frozen embryos
were in limbo
at the time
and would no longer
be harvested for their stem cells.
Evidently

it was a religious thing
to not help
grown men with spinal cord injuries
walk again,
or infertile women conceive.
But I couldn't wait to get through that state.

And the craving for crawdads?
It's all but vanished.

Paired with An 'Approachable' Wine

Approach me if you want,
you bitch of bacchus-ecstasy!

I'll unsay what I said during our last revelry.
You're a godawful red blend of sulphur and sorbate

and the date of your uncorking's
gone straight to my head.

I'm off to bed among the noxious weeds, naked
like your sculpture with its blackened genitalia.

A thick darkness descends
and the eucalyptus hints

a coming-on to complicate things. There's an intimacy
of two or three beneath the canopy—

and *What to pair?* has a sort of high-brow air about it.
Just know my compadres will arrive hammered

on spirits already plundered from *Saint Aloysius Bar & Grill*.
And some of us chew gum and cheese at the same time

we rub the Buddha's stomach for good luck.
Do you still want my keys? Last time

I checked they were to heaven's door,
but can I get another pour?

HORSERADISH

To make sauce of it's a big mistake.
A sauce would malign the vegetable.
A sauce would masque its true nature
as *Root* that must be wrenched from the dirt—
or perhaps a crowbar would do the job!

And yet, what kind of job would it be to exhume
a petrified child's crippled limb? Would it be proof?
Vindication for some innocent who'd been accused?
Extracting horseradish is similar work—
with parallel appeal . . .

Though your nostril-hairs may be singed, you will be cleared
of wrongdoing, and just by eating it raw, you cross
the Rio Grande—a pungent refugee (but free).
Are you fleeing persecution? This food is retribution.

An entire swarm of gnats will be consumed
before you have a bite of beef. The aroma will transport you
to labor-camps, where you'll convince *Victor Frankl*'s
of every age that he's smelling the fumes he'd smell
while landing on the moon.

It'll be as if you just missed the sacrifice of the ram,
who had been caught in the thicket, and slaughtered
in stead. You won't be dead, not yet, but already . . .
the embers will settle in the cleft between sweet
and sour. You'll be rescued by bitterness, back
from the depths of too much intoxicating pleasure.

And every meal will now be measured by
the terrestrial tinge on the tongue.

MIDDLING

"I could make prayers or poems on and on . . ."
—VASSAR MILLER, *IF I HAD WHEELS OR LOVE*

I could never have been Catholic
like this—reciting prayers by rote,
counting off calories like rosary beads,
slurping down the back-wash
from a common cup, gaging
on the cardboard wafer.

My exile began at *Pat's*
where a loogie landed on the sidewalk
and slippery as it was, after the purchase
of a cheesesteak, I stood tall
upon god-knows-who's saliva
and the mucous made me stick.

The *Plaza Cold Cuts* owner came by
eventually, and genuflecting
with his wad of cash, I was bought
and sold on the spot. Wind blew
through my nostrils and I bellowed
like a banshee.

The sirens of some ambulance beckoned me
to bless the cholesterol, or die trying.
I bent down and made a prayer
a poem and a poem a prayer.
An angel broke holy formation
and scavenged for leftovers.

Guided Tour

When Elisabeth Förster-Nietzsche sold tickets
to the parlor
where her brother reclined
with his goatee going fellatio
on the jib of his jaw

she justified herself with a knowing nod
to the murdered God,
a survivor of Zarathustra
and giddy in her grief
for thirty-five years.

Question: Could I have cared for the Priestess of
Eternal Germany . . . listened
to any self-loathing . . . held space
for the lonely fascism . . .
done her eulogy

without stuttering? It's possible I could have
wondered about their father's brain
disease, the horse beaten and
comforted in Turin's Square,
but I doubt it.

CONJUGATION, 1985

The gallantry of Rock Hudson (not his real name)'s
in doubt; and when in doubt

do what Doris Day did that day while I was taking
Kamikaze Greek at Princeton:

she stroked the cheek that seemed less gaunt,
and making pillow-talk in his left ear,

cemented their chemistry
before millions of viewers.

Conjugate for *voice, mood, tense, number*

—*and person.*

Transgender Spy Agency

"Germany has declared war on Russia.
Went swimming in the afternoon . . . "
—Franz Kafka, diary, August 2, 1914

As metamorphoses go
pronouns are dead giveaways,
which is why the dung beetle wakes up
colliding with *their* ottoman.

It was only days before retirement
when the agency called with some spiel
about reassigning
to active duty

where *they* could hide out among
he/him/his
she/her/hers
and no one would suspect

a nondescript thing
to arrange the table centerpiece
with apples once thrown
with vitriol.

So much so they'd become wedged
between the hard carapaces.
But there
they are—
shimmering with the other proud

56

fruits without a gender to speak of.
And not being acknowledged by fathers,
whose sex-organs swayed the course of history,
makes no difference.

The mothers, who wanted desk-duty
for their children, abhorred
the stench while tolerating
changes at the agency.

III. Being Hospitable to Grief

"Ah, Grief, I should not treat you
like a homeless dog . . .

I should coax you
into the house and give you
your own corner
a warm mat to lie on,
your own water dish . . . "

—DENISE LEVERTOV, FROM *TALKING TO GRIEF*

The Unruly Cogito-On-Board

My therapy dog snarls at every other
dog in the fuselage.
Elbow
to knee
to
armrest
in the last row.

I'd shut him up—"Caesar, shush!"
if it weren't for the ever-shrinking heads
in view before me
each
like a far-flung planet
with its own atmosphere
and hole in the ozone layer.

The lavatory door
sign says *Occupied*
as are the cloudy wisps
streaking by, where 'Descartes again
is sitting by the fire, dozing off . . . '

I doubt this. Therefore I think thus:
whatever non-material essence there is
pushes a button above my own
spherical head.

The blue-suited, be-speckled flight
attendant arrives. Why have I called?
How may I be helped? The fraud Freud said
I'd can't deny being
has run out of almonds.
My cup's empty of any beverage—
and I want leverage

or my dog's bound to bite!

Contrary to Theory

"Without friends, no one would want to live,
even if he had all the other goods."

—Aristotle, *The Nicomachean Ethics*

The canned goods, stolen by the Maine-woods hermit,
kept the lone man alive. He had no friends,
but evidence of his break-ins suggests
he knew many strangers,
and loved the chili-
beans out of
them.

SYNCHRONIZED FIRE-SETTING

We set a fire
on a windswept beach
close to the time
a sun would set
by crumpling
up the day's
newspaper
and striking
a match.

Each flame itself
rebelled, becoming
indifferent to the task
and we sipped
from the flask
we brought to
a continent's edge
and jeered at
stars arriving late.

SMOKING HELPS YOU THINK

Once lit and burning
your *Marlboro Lites* leave a perfect hole
in the dingy drape.

At dusk, I see the fierce embers as you inhale.
When that pinhole of flame goes dark
I can't even tell if you're still behind it,
holding your breath.

No matter. One puncture per pistil
of Black-Eyed Susan. One pressure point of nonchalance.
One obsidian epitaph so spot-on the abyss will be missed
with each tick of hands going 'round
the Roman-numeraled clock.

Each curlicue thinks a thought
not thought the whole way through.
Holy Smokes! To the highest heaven!

A Boat Bought with a Hole In It Becomes a Memory, and Works Just Fine

The wooden innards of the hull are exposed
but the skeleton's sound.

I'm about to stand upon the cushions of the back seat and leap
into the brackish water.

On the Sassafras all day
the outboard's churned up a vanilla milkshake
and I've gargled the white froth
like a gargoyle among pigeons.

These are my blood relatives, and the festivities are just
beginning.

Soon my father will toss an anchor in the air,
and the attached rope will drift on the wakes
we've created.

My mother, whose never learned to swim, will say I can't go
on a full stomach. Instead I'll stuff a pebble up my nose
and stare into a boiling pot.

The bow of the boat will be wedged in the same mucky bottom
I've felt before, squishing between my toes.

Thighs will rot,
breasts putrefy
and—
as chicken's always the best bait
for blue claw crab—
my brothers and sisters will have no choice
but to allow
additional time in the sun.

Emotional Purge

"...to these preventatives of disease may be added a gentle sweat
obtained by warm drinks, or gently opening the bowels by means of
one, two, or more of the purging pills."

—INSTRUCTIONS FROM DR. BENJAMIN RUSH, AS RECORDED
IN *THE JOURNALS OF LEWIS & CLARK*, JUNE 11, 1803

For me to tell you
no one knew what to do with their feelings
wouldn't be quite accurate. I could guess,
I suppose. I suppose I could guess
as to what collective, all encompassing,
sort of emotion passed through
the tourists of Lo Lo Pass
as we discovered
where *Discovery* had peed out their mercury-poisoning,

but the only honest thing to say is—
I, for one, traced a fascination with my sadness
all the way to the *Exxon* station restroom—
where, it turned out, I needed to buy
something ... anything ... maybe
some pumpkin seeds ... or maybe
a *Clark* bar
to gain access
and for which I needed a key
chained to a plastic Triceratops
(presumably so I wouldn't run off
with it) to unlock the door.

And so, I admit to being sad while in the process
of emptying my bladder of all the coffee I drank
on the way to arriving here,
which is probably more information that you needed
to read in this poem

about western expansion and the settling of the frontier.
But there you go.

CHAPLAIN@UVULA

1. Try It On

"And we: spectators, always, everywhere,
turned toward the world of objects, never outward.
It fills us. We arrange it. It breaks down.
We rearrange it, then break down ourselves."

—RAINER MARIA RILKE, *THE EIGHTH ELEGY* IN *DUINO
ELEGIES*

The room's a menagerie of stuffed animal heads and Nazi helmets
    on display.
I step from the doorway, identify myself
as chaplain and loiter a while
next to the man's wheelchair.
His urine bag sags by the violet
violence of his swollen ankles.
I smile and tell him
I'm there to listen.
He tells me
he doesn't want prayer—
there's no proof of anything
else—and *Would you look*
at Clint Eastwood? Man,
he's so young. I turn
and spy the actor's dark
sideburns and his cock-
sure gait. There's
dust vibrating
from the T.V.

speakers

(as the sound's turned up really loud).

I sit on the ottoman and watch the cowboy lay out his adversary
with a punch to the face.

In my hand is a book of psalms and prophets, all written by Jews.

Swastika's hang from the ceiling like mistletoe.

There's a North African pith with a sweat stain along the inner lining.

To build trust, I can try it on.

2. Antlers

You'll be pleased to know
a family of deer wandered by
the trailer as I knocked. When
you yelled 'Come in,' I bowed
all eight chakras before taking
your shots to the meatiest
part of my forehead.

3. Atoll At Ease

In a posture later described as men before urinals—
abreast and looking bemused—neither up nor down—
neither side to side—but gawking straight at *Why
are you looking here? The real joke's in your hand*—
it was accomplished: the phalanx on-deck broke ranks.
Their scaffolding of pant-legs
disassembled, their dark glasses doffed . . .
And thus the lagoon of our incontinence
seemed at ease. I heard the story from an eye-

witness dying of gag-reflex. Each time
(because there's nothing left to do)
he finger-navigates a web-site
the portobellos morph into the old ticker-tape parade.

If the higher-ups hadn't mega-phoned their caution he might've helped
himself to the abundance of coconut half-shells
laid to waste.

But he came home with merely the name
of a two-piece bathing suit for voluptuous women
who'd like their flesh exposed to
as much glory as there ever might be.

4. Maneuvers at the Care Facility

The photographed girl is soon to ski Priest Lake
    but given the entire, sprawling body can be quite ferocious
    and unforgiving when the wind whips up
    and the white-caps arise
    to greet one another,
        and when they bow down in their primordial gesticulations,
    she'll stick with a small fringe
    and call it good
    for the reminiscence churning
    always, deep below
    and long before the ice-dam broke,
    and in breaking, how it combed the terrain
    like the scalp of this beauty, who's outlived all others
    framed here, around the floating dock.

Even that young buck who idles his engine is gone into shadows,
and even the daughters have dipped toes into waters
all their own. The event clings to a nail nearest
the *Do Not Resuscitate* sign on the wall.
She's emaciated and ready
to taste the lake.

I flounder around for finger-holds on her vacant hand and grip it.
From where the mystery once frothed into wake after wake
she pulls my arms from their sockets.

4. Cracked Ribs

The paramedics had pounded his chest
like the sun going down on the horizon—
and that's where he should have died, he said—

on the skyline,
overlooking the city.
Not here,

amid these contraptions. And what I could do
with my pocket-size Bible was wipe my ass with it
on my way out the door.

A spouse has been saying, "We talked about this,
remember?
And now you're going to know before I do."

5. Matriarch

The daughter with whom she was living
her last days died, and she forgot
how sons don't call nearly enough
but yacht around the Mediterranean,
hobnobbing with caviar connoisseurs
like it was nobody's business.

Not to fret. Someone will come by
to ogle her unrelenting shapeliness.

6. Auto Parts

You scribbled the parts I still needed
on the back of some old billing statement.
I made the run to the Memory Unit and couldn't find a single one.
It was embarrassing to ask Mary to pray for us *alleged* sinners.
Many of the wheelchair-seated
wanted to move closer
to the windows.

I found the fix in the vast space behind the garage:
a myriad of corroded heaps,
metallic surfaces you had wept upon,
inflicted your torque upon,
crevices carburetors once occupied
in degrading stillness,
entire engine blocks from which melting
chunks of snow had dripped into your eyes
needed their entropy

blessed. I returned to the hour of your death
and you'd forgotten you sent me.

Mary though
was pretty at prayer—looking
like that actress you loved from Romeo & Juliet—

in the furrows of your brow.

7. Chaplain@Uvula

I looked up *uvula*
after the fact

but found the abyss around it
more culpable
for letting the soul escape.

The red-faced sentry then leaned back
against the larynx
and told the tongue to stand down. It was no use.

> Far from the rally point, a bloodied parachute snagged in the
> hedgerow.
> A punching bag was knocked from the trainer's fierce grip.
> A death-defying trapeze prodigy flung herself upside-down
> one last time.

And no, I'm not getting paid to stare into this gaping mouth

any longer
although I do

hold vigil. And when it's closed,
keep watch for any eyelid
twitch.

IV. Not-Knowing

"In this, my half-rest,
Knowing slows for a moment,
And not-knowing enters, silent,
Bearing being itself,
And the fire dances
To the stream's
Flowing."

—THEODORE ROETHKE, FROM *THE ABYSS*

ASYMPTOMATIC CARRIERS

I found my doppelgänger
near the front entrance
of *Assisted Living.*

Beneath the skies' unforgiving
downpour, he appeared the malingerer
who belonged and wouldn't go
without a light for very long.

The doors opened automatically
and as he wheeled himself inside
I said *Hello*
while ducking to eye-level.

Wanting religion
a stray pigeon flew above both our heads
and fluttered about the atrium.

Staff descended and ascended
with clipboards and brooms
upon ladders.

I made my rounds,
returned to the doors

and found the man alighted,
preparing to say
Goodbye.

HITCHCOCK BLONDE

They pecked the grounds for left-over grief
and flew off en masse
to terraces
above the oldest graves.

A spade-carrying Hitchcock follows and frames
the raptors in his lens.
Any prayers left dangling
from talons and beaks

now splay translucent in the sepia sun.
An icy blonde returns to kneel before
a phallic obelisk and performs
her petite mort on cue.

Does vertigo ensue?

BOTTLE DANCE

"Why should I tell you what the Good Book says?"
—TEYVE, *FIDDLER ON THE ROOF*

It happens
as the nurse attends
to bed sores: as the clavicle
upholds the covenant and the canopy,
the Hasidic head balances the old
bottle.   Tradition has it—

the thing's
bound to break

but not yet—while
the dance is being performed
the dust is being kicked up from the floorboards—
as the cameras roll and the clarinet fades—
before the director says *Cut!*

A Prayer for the Young Dead Who Never . . .

Not to indulge in all the co-morbidities
but in passing their memorials

I spy *procreate*
mastubate
consummate
fornicate
reprobate
annihilate . . .

and the list will never culminate.

> *Dear God, who in your wisdom*
> *made us bodies who relate:*
> *will you always sedate*
>
> *and make the senses dumb?*
>
> *Or will you fail to titillate the virgin dead*
> *with nothing less than a lurid katydid . . .*

INHIBITION LOST

> " ... in the resurrection they neither marry
> nor are given in marriage ... "
>
> —MATTHEW 22:30 (NRSV)

When the soulmate no longer pants to paradise
rhythms— her jowls jiggling—her jaws gaping wide—

the limousine arrives and takes him to plaid
pajamas he never owned
being laid out on the bed.

Turning twelve again
the daughter scoffs at accusations.
He's just a *grabby kind
of guy,*

always adjudicated
favorably to a fault.
Just look at the laminated *Certificate of Achievement*
and the Hawaiian lays
lauding that crystalline grin.

Sackcloth and ashes?
Please. Even the med-tech slaps him
on the back, *Atta boy,* as the asses are accessed
for firmness.

And yet
if there's a rude awakening
someday—any day now—

if his wife won't be his
perpetually alone—

so be it.

Neuropathy Eventually

These toes turning purple
once seemed orange in the sun.
I counted them on the Amalfi coast
by squinting and was satisfied

with a number—one more
than my fingers—which isn't bad.
Nearby newlyweds made no such
calculations, and watching

me watching them now I worry
if they caught the ferry back to Napoli . . .
or fucked themselves
beneath the cliff face

like driftwood in the surf.
Consider the pounding it takes
to become dust. One minute
you're leafing out on a limb

and the next you're awash
with briny rocks and sand—
and before you can stand
on your own nerve endings

toes assume the nacre
of shucked oyster shells. But
upon your bed of nails
some blanched pearls

eventually.

MUDSLIDES

All night long mudslides.
Mud slides all night long. A tree's
likely to uproot in this wind.
And given the storm's racket
neither one of us can sleep
in the cabin like we once could.

A few small mice (we're guessing)
scamper inside the walls
and with my eyes shut tight
I let their quiet sex tide me over.
Later the cramps in our calves we have
in our hip-joints as well.

A light switch won't turn on
the light. Not a single outlet has power going to it.
The fusebox is futile. That elderly woman
I met from low-income housing
enters my mind's eye . . . She speaks with
a Norwegian lilt

about her Lutheran baptism
when the slope begins to lean
perpendicular
to the window-frames.
My hands search for your hips
and find a steering wheel.

Hospice Chaplain, Interrupted

"For he has grown tired of amazing things."
—Larry Levis, *To a Wren on Calvary*

1.

Yes, it's you
disguised in your mother's adoring
pizza preparation.

Sprinkled with ptarmigan
(which is a known pathogen)
the picture on the box does it justice.

All things will put hair on your chest
as God intends you to live
without miracles.

And suddenly
the bridle-high flowing of blood
Hal Lindsey wrote about in that Armageddon

book is downplayed in the media.
The sleep-apnea of your therapist
redacts with black

all the Jungian boogies
from your spiritual acumen.
Why grieve the ghost

your stint as a late-night host
becomes when the show's shut down?
Eat the left-over crusts

while the car's still idling
by the idol factory.
Have you never read what David did?

2.

He entered the Kuerners
house (once painted by Wyeth)
and made himself a silhouette
in the candle-lit window.

The priests squatting there
owned dogs that marked territory
on the fieldstone facade night and day.
You weren't there long

before reading the riot act,
which is standard operating procedure
for institutions lasting more than
a hundred years;

and then, of course, the clerics scattered
into the hills
from where their help would come
(in the nick of time) but didn't.

Time was like a dog-leash after that
but even David's shadow failed to
curb the beasts to anyone's satisfaction
or feeling of just desserts.

And that's when you fed them simulacra.
Or rather—you brushed them into the painting
to give it texture. Everyone in the gallery seemed
pleased, and your own father sang

praises from the point of view of fire.
Plus he always loved dogs,
which is a good sign
for any occasion.

It signifies the tether in your happenstance—
and nothing all that genetic.

3.

But you remember Shirley,
who had three strokes before passing
the peace with her hands
extended and quivering.
Liturgically

Leslie Nielsen had a field day
with that one-liner from *Airplane!*
—and God must've granted permission:
*In the sure and certain hope of the resurrection
to eternal life . . . . "Don't call me, Shirley!"*

What a day to jump off the end of the pier
and into her open grave. Not a single orbital bone
batted an eye. Not the slightest
crack of a rib. The mourning husband
spoke a final word in French

for he'd taught it at *Lewis & Clark*
for decades. You lost your place
in the script—a _____ where
her name's inserted—
and a breeze made the pages flutter.

To commend anyone at that point
would be a feral cat's leap
into the dumpster
adjacent to the columbium.
If the banquet's a bust
at least there's a remnant to lick
from the can of
Chicken of the Sea.

V. An Open-Ended Sort of Closure

"Oh never mind, Jesus Christ, my father
And my uncles dug a hole in the ground,
No grave for once. It is going to be hard
For you to believe: when I rose from that water

A little girl who belonged to someone else,
A face thin and haunted appeared
Over my left shoulder, and whispered, Take care now,
Be patient, and live."

—James Wright, from *The Old WPA Swimming Pool
in Martin's Ferry, Ohio*

Estate Sale for the Neurologically Disordered

"There was here a veritable consecration, hopeful and animating, of the
earth's gifts, of old dead and dark matter itself ... "
—Walter Pater, *Marius the Epicurian*

Unlike the *Chia-Pets* with their chia
growing like hair from one of Whitman's old graves
(or like Whitman himself when he lived in Camden)—
and unlike the set of *Ginzu Knives*
outflanking the flank steak—
a thingamajig catches the sunlight

just right, just as
the auctioneer pauses to clear his throat.

There's an intrinsic value the hand of
the bidder knows,
independent and severed
from one's own intentionality
and wishes,

which means certain calamari
dishes possess their users' appendages
before even being
ready-at-hand.

Thus tentacles, rehearsing their old attachments,
raise themselves to secure what's offered.

No one's guilty of hoarding here.
The auction's the opposite of rigged—
and into the drawer
goes another
thingamajig.

SPOILED

The residue
left from the micro-plastics
entering our systems
will be the lazy fog
of guessing

at innuendos. And
notice the future
tense
because they *will* be coming
to suburban

America already,
but not yet,
in the form of chores
listed, but deferred
for other honey's

to do
when they get around to it.
For example, a spouse
may want the wood
stacked

near the backdoor
in case of snow . . . And—
I'll give you the backdoor
will come the reply
under the breath

of each partner in life.
The resulting strife will creep
endemically
euphemism by euphemism
until

winter sets in and the winds
whisper a straightforward
meaning.

It won't register a thing,
and the house will grow
cold, and the wood will
lie strewn about
like the lingerie once
imagined around
the unmade bed.

AKEDAH REDUX

My son stood at the base of the stairs
in the manse with its old wallpaper
and said his room was *broken*,
which it was—and not just
the window pane, which had a crack
in it, and would need replacing
by the Trustee Committee of
First Presbyterian. And yet, once fixed
the four-year-old said goodbye to
the bemused dreams and shrieking
nightmares he had in that small town . . .
And so we came to a big city's
sprawling suburbs, and my son said,
there's a nuclear power plant nearby
spewing ominous vapors into
the blue sky, and we received
thyroid-blocking pills, also blue,
in the mail just in case of meltdown,
which never happened, but could have.
And the church there grew among
the invasive weeds off Route 422,
which we'd take after a decade
to go back west again,
and my son, before
we packed the van, said
he'd written a poem for his friends
to remember him by . . . but
the poem so frightened well-
meaning parents, a few

feared a teenage suicide, and
my son said he didn't mean
anything by it, and went to college
where God didn't exist after all,
and he called (a little drunk
by the sound of
his voice)
and said,
Remember when my room
was broken—
have we ever spoken since?

BUTT DIAL

The ringtone for you is by Neil Young
and after swiping your face
on the chorus

I can barely make out which body
part has called.

There's a gang of drum-beats
pummeling the air where you evidently are.
Our shared-location technology says
it's *The Globe.*

And now your mother and I are crying out.
She in particular ups her volume.

I picture a cell tower
atop a mountain
pinging with the raucous, high-pitched
din, and dogs bellowing for miles around.
Even bats, soaring with their sonar,
attend to the screech and fly into trees.

We hush ourselves and listen
as if waiting between lightning flashes and thunder.

A garbled series of guffaws.
A muffled clinking of glass.
The *Om* of the Universe . . .
But no reply.

How We'll Age Together's Hard to Know

I see us in line for breakfast,
the bodies we once ate
to sustain
no longer in need.

There's a rectangular ounce of quartz
before our feet, slightly
smoothed at the corners,
and with our slip-on shoes
we take turns nudging it through
a labyrinth of shadows.

> Back
> and
> forth
> between us.

Breezes from a gray ocean
tussle the tassels of window curtains,
which are there to make the hemorrhaging
desire stop, and slantwise the sun
arrows light through seams
in their fabric.

You smell *Pachebel's Canon in D*
warming like bread
from the house next store.

I remark on what a good whiffer
you've always had, and rest
my four-fingered hand on your beauty.

We wait. We want. We wait.

To All the Corpses Still Bestowing the Secret Great Commission

Having made our visit—here's the (newly revised)
overwhelming
question:

> Was it the opal pendant that deceived
> or the esoteric writing of the creed?

And as a follow-up:

> Was it Constantinople that believed
> or the lovers who conceived
>
> that leaves the body feeling prone?
> that suckles praise from every stone?

Baptizing Sturgeon

It will be the backsliding feat
of millennia

when you grab the dinosaur-tail
with both hands

and let go
(as justice demands)

only to find
gutted to the spine

the light that brought
you here.

(Or Does It?)

The doorbell rings. (Or does it?)
You're dozing not far away

in a brown leather recliner
to which the bare flesh
of your upper arms
adheres because of
climate-change lately.

You've heard a sound in your dreamy
    half-waking state

      of mind.
You intend to rise and answer the door.

Approaching the threshold from within
(because where else would you be)
you're preparing to greet—

but there's no one

there to meet.

Or is it—they're simply far away

                             from you?

BIBLIOGRAPHY AND WORKS CITED

"Airplane." Paramount Home Video, 1980.

Cohen, Richard A. "Page 32." *Face to Face with Levinas*, State University of New York Press, Albany, 1986.

Davis, Jr. *Levinas*, University of Notre Dame Press, 1997, pp. 132–132.

Derrida, Jacques, et al. *Adieu to Emmanuel Levinas*. Stanford University Press, 1999.

Descartes, Rene. *Meditations on First Philosophy*. Hackett Publishing Co, 1993.

Hagglund, Martin. *This Life*. Profile Books Ltd, 2019.

Harrison, Robert Pogue. *The Dominion of the Dead*. University of Chicago Press, 2010.

Heidegger, Martin, and Martin Heidegger. *Being and Time*. Harper.

Kearney, Richard. *Anatheism: Returning to God after God*. Columbia University Press, 2011.

Kierkegaard, Soren. *The Diary of Soren Kierkegaard*. Citadel Press, 2000.

Kockelmans, Joseph J. *Phenomenology: The Philosophy of Edmund Husserl and Its Interpretation*. Anchor Books, 1986.

Levinas, Emmanuel. *Time and the Other: (And Additional Essays)*. Duquesne University Press, 2008.

———. *Totality and Infinity an Essay on Exteriority*. Duquesne Univ. Pr. Usw., 1969.

———. *God, Death, and Time*. Stanford Univ. Press, 2002.

———. *Otherwise than Being, or, beyond Essence*. Duquesne University Press, 2016.

Long, Thomas G. *Accompany Them with Singing: The Christian Funeral*. Westminster John Knox Press, 2013.

May, Todd. *Death*. Routledge, 2016.

McGilchrist, Iain. *The Master and His Emissary: The Divided Brain and the Making of the Western World*. Yale University Press, 2010.

Otto, Rudolf. *The Idea of the Holy*. Boon Do Publishing, 1987.

Pentaris, Panagiotis. "Chapter 8 and 9." *Religious Literacy in Hospice Care: Challenges and Controversies*, ROUTLEDGE, S.l., 2020.

Peters, Edward N. "God Bless Fr. LaCuesta." *The Catholic World Report*, Dec. 2018.

Press, Gerald A. *Plato's Dialogues: New Studies and Interpretations.* Rowman & Littlefield, 1993.

Ramsey, K.J. "There's No Shame When A Miracle Doesn't Come." *Christianity Today*, Dec. 2019.

"A Service of Witness to the Resurrection of the Jesus Christ." *Book of Common Worship*, Westminster John Knox Press, Louisville, KY, 2018.

Shanks, Andrew. 'What is Truth? Towards a Theological Poetics. Routlege, London, UK, 2001.

Tisdale, Sallie. "Out of Time; the Unbecoming of Self." *Harpers*, Mar. 2018.

Wright, James, et al. "Saint Judas." *Selected Poems*, Farrar, Straus and Giroux, New York, 2005.